SONGS FROM GLEE

COLLECTION FOR YOUNG VOICES

Featured in the Twentieth Century Fox
Television Series GLEE

Original GLEE Arrangements
by Adam Anders and Tim Davis

Adapted for publication by Tom Anderson

TABLE OF CONTENTS

ISBN 978-1-4234-9287-0

7777 W. BLUEMOUND RD. P.O. BOX 13819 MILWAUKEE, WI 53213

Visit Hal Leonard Online at
www.halleonard.com

Recorded by REO SPEEDWAGON
and Featured in the Twentieth Century Fox Television Series GLEE

CAN'T FIGHT THIS FEELING

Original *GLEE* Arrangement
by ADAM ANDERS and TIM DAVIS
Adapted for Publication by TOM ANDERSON

Words and Music by
KEVIN CRONIN

Featured in the Twentieth Century Fox Television Series GLEE

DON'T STOP BELIEVIN'

Original *GLEE* Arrangement
by ADAM ANDERS and TIM DAVIS
Adapted for Publication by TOM ANDERSON

Words and Music by STEVE PERRY,
NEAL SCHON and JONATHAN CAIN

small-town girl,___ liv-in' in___ a lone-ly world.___

Dah Dah Dah Dah Dah Dah Dah Dah Dah Dah Dah Dah

She took the mid-night train___ go-in' an-y-where.___

Dah Dah Dah Dah Dah Dah Dah Dah Dah Dah Dah Dah

opt. Solo 2

Just a cit-y boy,___ born and raised in

Dah Dah Dah Dah

G   D   Em7

south De - troit.___ He took the mid - night train__ go - in'

end Solo 2 **26**

an - y - where.___

guitar solo

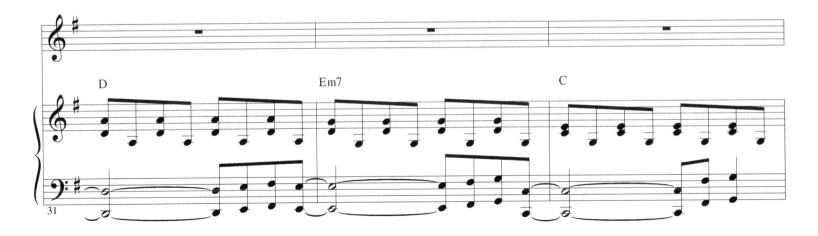

Some will win,___ some will lose,___ some were born__ to

sing the blues.___ And, oh the mov - ie nev - er ends;___ it goes

on and on___ and on___ and on.___ Stran - gers___

wait - ing___ up and down the boul - e - vard,___ their

shad - ows___ search - ing___ in the night.___

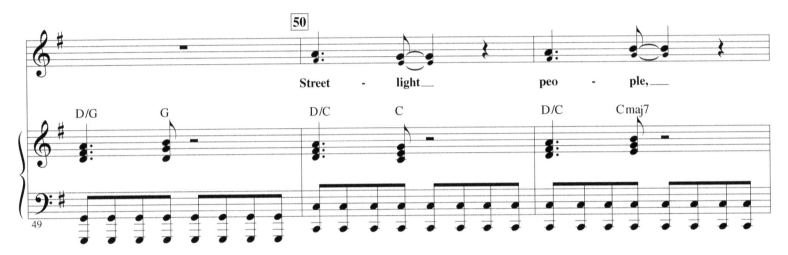

Street - light___ peo - ple,___

liv - ing just to find e - mo - tion, hid - ing___

some - where___ in the night.___

58 **Drive to end**

Don't__ stop be - liev - in'.__ Hold on to the

G   D   Em7

feel - in',__ street - light peo - ple.__

C   G   D

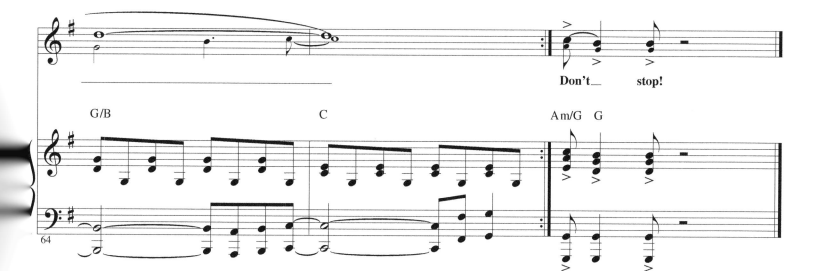

Don't__ stop!

G/B   C   Am/G G

The 1984 #1 Pop Hit by VAN HALEN
and Featured in the Twentieth Century Fox Television Series GLEE

JUMP

Original *GLEE* Arrangement
by ADAM ANDERS and TIM DAVIS
Adapted for Publication by TOM ANDERSON

Words and Music by DAVID LEE ROTH,
EDWARD VAN HALEN, ALEX VAN HALEN
and MICHAEL ANTHONY

* "Migh's well" = Might as well

Recorded by BILL WITHERS
and Featured in the Twentieth Century Fox Television Series GLEE

LEAN ON ME

Original *GLEE* Arrangement
by ADAM ANDERS and TIM DAVIS
Adapted for Publication by TOM ANDERSON

Words and Music by
BILL WITHERS

Some - times in our lives___ we all have pain,___ we all have sor-

- row.___ But, if we are wise,___ we know that there's_

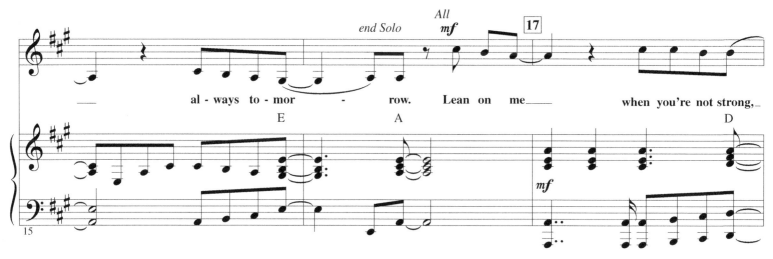

al - ways to - mor - row. Lean on me___ when you're not strong,_

and I'll be your friend,_ I'll help you car - ry on;___

for it won't be long___ 'til I'm gon - na need___ some - bod - y to lean___

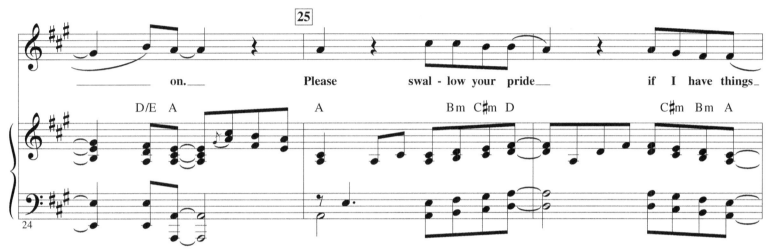

___ on.___ Please swal - low your pride___ if I have things___

you need to bor - row;___ for no one can fill___

___ those of your needs___ that you won't let___ show.

* If melody is out of range, sing notes in parentheses.

5/10

Recorded by QUEEN
and Featured in the Twentieth Century Fox Television Series GLEE

SOMEBODY TO LOVE

Original *GLEE* Arrangement
by ADAM ANDERS and TIM DAVIS
Adapted for Publication by TOM ANDERSON

Words and Music by
FREDDIE MERCURY

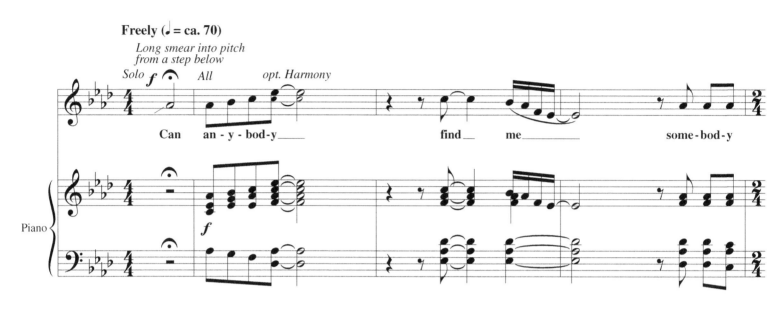

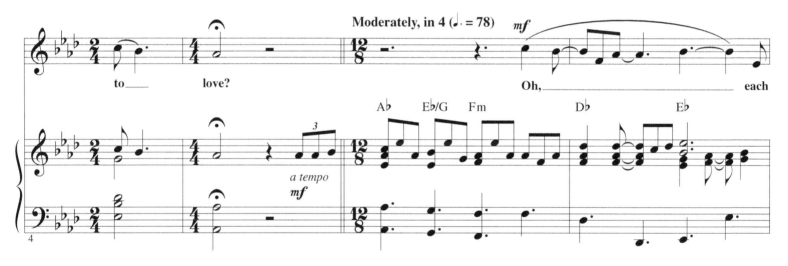

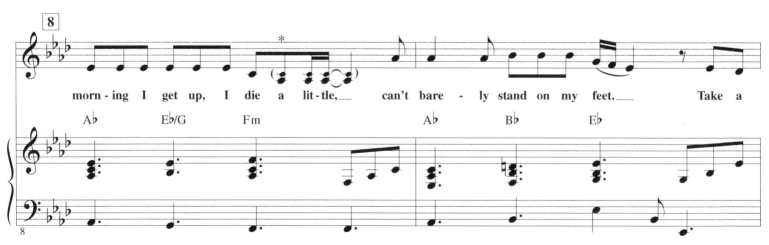

* If melody is out of range, sing notes in parentheses.